New Age Man
Con Game Over

15 Ways Guys Con Women

Beware
Women Stay One Step Ahead

By

Dr. Marilyn Marlow
(The Sex Shark Buster!)

DEDICATION

To all the Women in the world

who have had pseudo love,

and deserve so much more!

ACKNOWLEDGEMENT

Without a doubt there are caring and loving men in

the world. This guide gives recognition to those kind of

wonderful men. All women that have one of these men in

their lives are hopefully grateful he is part of her life!

Knowing there are conscionable men like that out there has

inspired this writing. Also, eminent thanks to Diane whose

encouragement has helped made available

this information for women.

QUOTATIONS OF LOVE

"Nothing, no better than Love, if for Love itself."

"If Love knocks, let Love in, when heart felt!"

"Be wise, nor fool, the man who uses Love as a tool;
for this Love is not!"

"Beware of he that leer thee, with a promise of Love."

"My heart has felt many a liar, for Love to be;
but thy seek still!"

"Arms wide open, if to embrace real Love!"

"Many call Love, but heat of physical passion;
this Love is false!"

"To ponder upon Love, is to definitely want Love true."

"Love hold me in your hand, for thy time of Love is at hand."

"Love has yet to arrive, but the quest lives on."

Author

CONTENTS

UNDERSTANDING THE NEW AGE MAN

Driven by an insatiable appetite for sex, no one woman can ever satisfy the New Age man. He is a live missile, explosive at any moment, anywhere, and anyway as long as he has a willing victim (woman) at his disposal. He is on the brink of sex all the time, because this is an easy, efficient, and effective sexual mechanism that these men have physiologically built in.

Some of these men can have multiple ejaculations with one sexual encounter. It takes little stimulation to achieve their sexual ends, as long as they can con new women into participation. Since his sexual appetite is unsatisfiable, he requires a constant, fresh supply of women. This man has the edge over most women for sexual pleasure.

New Age men are coerced by their innate nature, and will go to any extent or extreme to achieve the sexual ends. In a sense they are sexual psychopaths, because sexually they are totally amoral and asocial characters according to today's standards by definition of these words. He is self-absorbed and keeps undercover his unconstrained sexual drive for lust and physical pleasure.

This man is usually immature and undeveloped emotionally; probably emotional wiring left over from prehistoric times. Crude and dense would best describe the New Age man's emotional relationship mentality even though some of these men are academic geniuses. Make no mistake, he is a sex shark!

WHAT MAKES HIM TICK AND HIS MOTIVES

The New Age man is diabolically insincere and will use all kinds of tactics to seduce and control his victims. He does this by preying on a woman's weaknesses and vulnerabilities to achieve sexual conquest. This man is not in the game to bring anything to a woman, although at first he appears to be exactly what she needs and wants in a man. He is only in it for his physical pleasure at the moment.

He may appear to be there for the woman in the beginning, but this is just a façade. This is how he wins a woman over and reels her in, but the reality is to beget his own sexual gratification and nothing else. The New Age man wants to achieve his sexual ends with as many women as he can as quickly as possible in his life. The more women and the faster he can get a woman sexually the better. Nothing in the world matters to this man except SEXUAL CONQUESTS! These are unconscionable men with a sex drive that goes way beyond the normal rim.

Because of the sexual revolution of the 1960's and women believing in sexual equality, women have become sexual prey to these kinds of men. They truly believe a woman is only good for one thing, "SEX." Lust is OK if both partners are aware that's just what it is, but this is not the case when getting involved and becoming a victim of the sex shark. He makes a woman believe whatever it is she may want with him, by offering women their fantasies and dreams. He is a master of deception, lies, and sexual fraud. A con man duping women out of their sex and everything else he can – even her own sanity – if she lets him in and he gets control over her, which by the way, CONTROL IS HIS FORTE. The reason he does this is so he can have her sex anytime he desires sex from this victim.

The New Age man only wants sexual favors from women, but he is very pretentious and will make a woman believe whatever it is she thinks he is or wants with him. In reality, he is contrary to her beliefs, and pretending to be agreeable, keeping her hooked until some new game comes along, and then it's off to his next sexual conquest. The reason he does this is very simple – The New Age man is a glutton for control and sex!

HOW TO DETECT THE NEW AGE MAN IMMEDIATELY

New Age man has long pervaded society, but with today's text on seduction, and given the current attitude on gender sexual equality, and birth control pills, women feel free to let down their guard concerning actions they believe no longer carry serious consequences; these women are easy prey. These men are no longer branded as bad because they mislead a woman for only their own selfishness of sexual gratification. Males have backing from other men and are no longer judged as having bad intentions for women. Instead men are viewed by other men as "the man" or as getting to live out most every man's life-long sexual fantasy – as many women as quickly as possible.

Men without this selectively innate nature DO NOT KNOW how horrific and defiled the New Age man is, because a normal man does not possess this innate chemistry and can not understand that this man is a sexual psychopath. Normal men desire the intimacy that a committed relationship inspires. Average men cannot fathom what New Age men will do psychologically and physically to a woman to sexually prey on her.

This is BIG GAME for the New Age man, in that, women have sexual goods that these men desire. The New Age man wants a woman's sexual goods for nothing, or as cheaply as possible – with NO emotional or monetary investment, so he uses psychological tricks and sometimes physical force instead. Remember that women are called "street walkers" or "call girls" who receive money for sex. The New Age man wants a woman's sexual goods as if she walks the street or is a call girl, but free of charge.

These are the signals the man you just met is a New Age man, a sexual psychopath, and a woman's worst nightmare. The New Age man loves the sexual game – that's all. He will never love a woman. The tactics he employs/uses on women are complicated.

1. Reversal role: makes a woman do something a man should do.

2. Mimics her words; monkey hears, monkey says.

3. Mirrors her actions; monkey sees, monkey does.

4. Reflects her opinions and feelings; stands in her shoes, sees the world from her point of view, so he can use her reflections of opinions and feelings on and against her.

5. Parrots her ideas and beliefs; Polly want a cracker? Polly want a cracker?

6. Insincerely, he uses fictitious, warm, tender words and a woman's own language; he knows a woman has a need for those kinds of words and her own language.

7. He uses sympathy; makes her feel sorry for him.

8. He keeps a woman guessing: What is he doing, when is he going to call, is he seeing someone else, does he care, etc., etc.?

9. The New Age man is usually innately selfish, therefore, he is a cheapskate; and he will only spend what he needs to keep the sexual favors coming from his victims.

10. He will try to make sexual jokes with/at a woman from the very first moment he speaks with her; he wants to establish sexual harmony with a woman from the start.

11. He is very agreeable with a woman in words only, but never pleasing. He goes along with what a woman says, but will never follow through doing anything for her. He will only do the things he wants. What she wants he will continually make her want from him. This is a form of control and power over her.

12. He will create triangles: Make a woman believe other women are pursuing him or someone else is in his life or he is attracted to another woman. This makes him appear more desirable.

13. He may act like a gentleman at first: Bows and kisses a woman's hand, or he is reserved and proper.

14. The New Age man is on the Internet dating services: His profile is devoid of personal reflection or feelings. He usually claims a very large income as a drawing card.

15. He wants a woman to renounce her life for him; he makes up fictitious stories as a way of getting her to do this, so he can control her.

EXAMPLES OF HIS TACTICS OR ACTIONS

He starts by breaking down a woman's defenses of protections, so he can penetrate her:

1. A REVERSAL ROLE; he gives a woman his phone number instead of taking hers. She might say, "I don't play that game," and if he is interested in her, he'll take her number instead. Beware, he may be only obliging her to start his game, so she should proceed with caution. Then, later on, after a woman gets involved with him, he'll make the woman pursue him for sex, as if he has the sexual goods instead of the woman. Then he'll refuse her, because he is on to some bigger, better, and new game, another woman! He will still keep his old victims on a string just in case he wants to use them again for sexual favors if his next, new victim doesn't work out as planned or just for a change in sexual partners. He's a master at using woman!

2. He MIMICS a woman's WORDS; says what she says. If he speaks with her on the phone or takes a woman out, (which is doubtful at this time, because this man does not want to spend money on a date unless she gives him sexual favors, and then, he'll spend only a miniscule amount, he has many women he must spend money on for their sexual favors) he will, in other words, say her words, but in a different manner or light. She might say, "OH, YOU'RE SO SWEET for caring for your old, sick mother," which is probably a lie to begin with. Then he may leave her a message the next day or tell her something like, "OH, YOU'RE SO SWEET that you better stay out of the rain, because SWEET things melt." Or he may ask her birthday, and she says, "It's January 16th." He may say, "Isn't that a coincidence, mine is July 16th" - when his is really July 18th. He mimics a woman's exact words, but they're applied to a different, most likely a fictitious situation or story. The New Age man will seldom use his own words. He is a horrific liar.

3. He will MIRROR a woman's ACTIONS; does what she does. She is on a date with him for the first time and she holds her drink/glass a certain way, so he holds his drink/glass that way or she leans forward, so he waits a minute and leans forward like she did. He mirrors a woman's actions. He's a real monkey!

4. He obtains a woman's REFLECTIONS, so he can use her perceptions to con her. He may tell a woman he is going to get a new car, either a new Lincoln or Cadillac, (which is a total lie) but he doesn't know which one he should get. He wants her reflection of her opinion and feeling about the car. She says, "I LOVE the SMALL, CLASSY new Cadillac, because it's the PERFECT car to me." The next time he speaks with her on the phone or in person, he'll use her exact words on her and say, "He LOVES how SMALL and CLASSY she is, just PERFECT for him." He reflects back her opinion or feeling in her EXACT words about the new car he said he was going to get (in reality

he had no intention of getting a new car, this was just a ploy he used to get her opinion or feeling) and uses her own words on her. This type of technique/action is psychologically dynamic in controlling a person (woman in this case) and making a person succumb to their wishes by making the person (woman) trust and even falling in love with the person (man in this case) by employing this technique. Remember a healthy person loves him/her self, so he is trying to be YOU! He uses this tactic for control, and getting sexual favors or anything else he may want from his victims. If a man begins reflecting back a woman's exact perception of her opinions and feelings in words, she better run away as fast as she can. This is a true sign he is not sincere, but only a TRICKSTER!!

5. He PARROTS a woman's IDEAS and BELIEFS. She may tell him she adversely disagrees with the president and war in Iraq. The New Age man will totally agree with her about the president and the war. Or she may tell him she believes all women should be treated equal as men in the workplace. He will tell her he believes all women should be treated equal as men in the work place too. She likes reading books - he likes reading books, she's Baptist – he's Baptist. Actually, in reality he's nothing but a BIG JERK who is a diabolical con man, seemingly to be in harmony with the woman's ideas and beliefs he is trying to seduce. He is trying to gain her trust by being agreeable and pull her into his net of deception. He will never say his true beliefs, because he has BAD INTENTIONS.

6. The New Age man uses a woman's LANGUAGE and WARM TENDER WORDS. He knows a woman has an innate need for words of this nature and to hear her own language. He will tell a woman he is very attracted to her and he wants to get to know her better or he needs her, or he is very fond of her, and if she asks him, "Do you love me?" He'll reply, "It's headed that way." He is insincere and doesn't mean a word of it. He will never tell

a woman he loves her or get in too deep emotionally, just enough to get a woman's sexual favors. He will say he is very romantic or the chemistry must be right, but what he really means is he wants to fuck her! The New Age man has mastered the art of using a woman's language and warm, tender words, insincerely, so he can pull her into his web and suck her dry.

7. He uses SYMPATHY to make a woman feel sorry for him. "My wife just died and this is all new to me," (what he means, is this woman is all new to him and he probably cheated on his wife for years) or "My old girlfriend was so cruel to me," or "It's been so long since I've been in a relationship." Actually, the New Age man has never been in a relationship and only the women he has victimized have been in the relationship with him. He may say it's been so long since he's had sex, but he always has sex with anyone he can. It has always been purely a sexual experience for him nothing more. He is cold, heartless, and empty without any capacity of getting involved emotionally in a relationship with any woman.

8. He wants to keep a woman GUESSING. Always wondering what he is doing and with whom? This keeps a woman intrigued and a captive victim of his for not knowing what's coming next. This man will never keep a date or time he is supposed to do something with a woman. This man will get a woman to commit to a date or time to do something with him, so he can deliberately break or change it. He will tell her he is coming over to repair the electrical plug he has promised to do for her for several months. She tells him she will make him lunch when he comes over to do that for her. Instead he calls at the last minute and tells her he was called into work and won't be able to do that for her. The woman is stuck with a lunch for two and him letting her down. After all, he must go into work. He will call up the last minute with all kinds of excuses to break the date or change the time. He isn't feeling well enough to go out or his hot water

isn't working, so he can't clean up, or an old friend from out of town has just called and wants to drop in to visit. He may want to make the date earlier or later depending on the circumstances he fabricates. The New Age man likes to use his job or work as the main excuse for breaking dates or changing times. He may say he will call at a certain time on a certain day, but he does NOT call then, or he will ask the woman when she would like him to call again, she says when, so he does NOT call then. If the woman confronts him on why he didn't call her then, he might say he fell asleep or he was unexpectedly busy at that time. He is a deliberate, undependable maniac trying to cause a woman as much turmoil and anxiety as possible.

9. The New Age man is INNATELY SELFISH and he is probably a CHEAPSKATE. He may make a woman believe he has money even if he doesn't by saying he drives a very expensive car or brag about his profession and income. This makes him more attractive financially. Regardless, if he has money or not, he will never lavish or treat a woman right. He will only spend enough money to keep a woman's sexual favors coming his way. He will take a woman to dinner or for drinks, bring her flowers, candy and small trinkets, but he will never consider a weekend trip, a nice piece of jewelry or a fur coat. He may promise a woman a ring, but when it comes time to go get it or pick it out, all of a sudden his friend will be in dire need of his help, so he can't go. This man is always on the hunt for bigger, better, and new game, so he limits his spending to a minimal. He must have enough to spend on his next sexual victim. What woman needs a selfish cheapskate?

10. He immediately throws SEXUAL JOKES or little sexual innuendos at a woman. He does this to establish sexual harmony with a woman from the start. Remember the faster the better. He figures if he can get her to conform to this behavior from the start, he's probably got her already. For example: The woman may ask,

24

"Why don't you have a cottage like your brother?" He answers, "Oh, when my father told me to get a lot, I didn't know he meant land." He makes remarks like, "One thrown over the shoulder is one missed," or he may ask, "I'm southern; would you like being southern by injection?" He may try getting a woman to participate in a sexual joke by standing up or using her hands or another body part. The New Age man is obsessed with sexual lust and it will show if a woman watches for it. He wants to seem funny, but his underlying motive is immediate sexual harmony. These jokes are meant to open a woman up immediately sexually, for sex with him. Remember, his only objective is to conquer a woman sexually as quickly as possible and use her as a sexual object for as long as he wants, and can use her when he wants to use her. He is an impertinent cad with an insulting disposition.

11. He is CHARMING, and AGREEABLE with anything a woman has to say, but will never do anything PLEASING for a woman. He will not do anything she wants or needs. The New Age man is all talk and will make all kinds of promises, but will never follow through. He WOOS a woman right to his bed without good intentions. He will only do what he wants or needs and expects the woman to jump at his every whim. What she wants he will continually make her want from him. This is a very frustrating situation to be in, so avoid his charm at all measures. If a man is not pleasing from the start, he's probably not interested in the woman, only the sex she has to offer. Talk is cheap! Dump him quick!

12. He creates TRIANGLES, making a woman wonder if he has another woman in his life. This makes him look more desirable if other women are interested in him and after him. He'll make a woman believe he has other avenues for sex or he is attracted to another woman. He may make a remark about another woman while he is on a date. He's trying to make his date jealous! Don't be fooled. It's just a façade to get a woman hooked on him and

in his bed for as long as he wants.

13. He may act like a perfect GENTLEMAN at first, but this is just a front. Deep down he is a brute and ruthless. He might bow and kiss a woman's hand and tell her he'd love to take her for dinner. He may tell the woman, he has never had the opportunity to take out such a beautiful brunette, redhead or blonde in his life before her. This is a blatant lie. He has taken out every kind of woman there is out there! He is trying to make the woman think she is special and he hasn't been around much. He is no gentleman, but a slick man with a tremendous amount of experience that knows how to use it. He has been with every women possible whenever the opportunity has presented itself!

14. He is signed up with the INTERNET DATING SERVICES, and he'll state only facts, such as what he likes. Usually his profile is short, devoid of feelings and reflection. He claims big income, $150,000. plus as an attraction feature, even though it's probably a lie. His statements could be ambiguous, for example: "Captain, looking for 1st mate," as his picture portrays him sitting on a big boat. This statement could simply mean he wants first (1st) time new women for mating. His whole scenario is misleading! Or he may say, "Looking for a life mate," which could suggest a life time mate, but this isn't what he means. His meaning is far less meaningful. What he has in mind is mating with different women throughout his life. Look out he is very clever at untruths!

15. He tries to make a woman renounce her own life for his. A woman may tell him she has plans for a certain day or going away for the weekend to visit her family. He'll have a comeback when she returns. He may say, "Oh, while you were gone an old girlfriend came from out of town to visit me and stayed the night, but nothing happened." Or he may say, "While you were gone my son came over and brought two young women over to drink and party at my house and they spent the night, but I went to bed

early and alone. He tries to make a woman sorry she has her own life, because this leaves him at bay without control over her. This tactic is a ploy used for controlling a woman from having her own life, by making her feel helpless when she makes decisions in her life. He uses this technique as a form of getting control over her. The woman made a decision and look what happened. He is just a liar trying to get control over her, by making her anxious about making decisions in her life for fear of what might happen for doing so.

PROTECT YOURSELF

If a man you meet mimics, reflects or parrots the words of your feelings, opinions, ideas and beliefs, and mirror your actions become suspicious and cautious. Pay attention to what you tell a man and remember the exact words you say to him. The New Age man cleverly keeps under wraps a superb memory for detail. He also may have an above average intelligence. You may become his next sexual conquest and victim if you are not aware of these facts and remember the words in your conversation with him.

Beware of any man who starts using your words immediately after speaking with him. If a man begins using your words on you, quickly as possible, get away from him. Also, he may ask you your feelings or to elaborate on how you feel about something. This is a definite sign he is searching for your opinions or feelings, so he can reflect them back to you. He is probably a New Age man only in it for sexual conquest and his own sexual gratification. These men are emotionally distant and closed. They are never open or honest about their feelings, because they are usually emotionally exempt or hiding how they really feel. Most women would be on guard if they knew his true feelings.

Do not be open, frank, or honest with this kind of man. Do not let him in! This information is what the New Age man feeds off of and needs to be successful in a sexual conquest. Being caught in his web will surely cause you great emotional turmoil and regret. These men are horrific characters with no scruples.

RID YOURSELF
FOREVER OF HIM

If a male acquaintance appears to be a New Age man and you want to know for sure before you proceed any further with him, give him a test. When casually conversing with him, mention that you wonder why more men cheat than women? Listen very carefully to what he says. If he answers something like, "Men have all the angles," or "It's easier for a man, if his job permits." It's very likely he is indeed... New Age.

Also, ask something, such as you wonder how a man can tell a woman is hot? Give him a moment, he'll love answering this one. He might say, "Just by the way she moves," or "Her movements tell it all or give it away." He'll make some comment about the way she moves. You're in trouble just for talking to this guy.

Tell him, you wonder how most men feel in general about women these days? A man who chases after women may say, "There isn't a woman I don't love," or "I love all women." Actually there is a contrary sentiment deep in his heart. The reality is the New Age man must really loathe women, because he wants to desecrate a woman's body by lusting after her and using her for sex and anything else he may want from her without giving anything in return.

Also, tell him (a story/fib), about an ex-boyfriend who picks up prostitutes on the street, and mention, "He's a dirty old pig." If he mimics your words, "Dirty old pig, unh??" Believe me, he probably picks up prostitutes too. You better bail out of this one as quickly as possible. Disease is an issue here!

HIS STATUS FACTOR

The New Age man is single, divorced, widowed, going steady, engaged or married. He is sexually amoral and asocial, so it doesn't matter if he is committed to a woman in any way. He doesn't distinguish between right and wrong when it comes to sex. He easily lives multiple lives without remorse. These men all have one thing in common, they are all on the hunt for new sexual experiences their whole lives anywhere or anytime, as long as they have a willing victim.

He is often older and very experienced. Some younger men practice such tactics from reading about seduction. Younger men are vulnerable to thinking lust is love and looking for their dream girl/woman to have a family with, because younger men are more idealistic. They marry and start families. Yet, this is an innate trait to be New Age and may become full-blown as he gets older if he is clever enough or he has above average intelligence. The more experience he has, the better he is at the game. That's why older men, usually over forty, are better and very skilled at this game. He has hands-on experience, literally, from trial and error. He has the con down to an art, a whole routine he pulls on women.

He arrives from all walks of life. He can be a salesman, a doctor or a whistle blower to state the least. If his job permits, and he is committed in any way to another woman, he will take full advantage of his availability by/from his job to get away and hunt for new victims and have sexual experiences. For instance: If he's a doctor, he may tell his wife/girlfriend he's on his way to the hospital for an emergency, or if he is on call for work he may say he was called into work or he has to work a double shift, or he has to show a house to a client! If he is married, and the woman he is on the hunt for knows he is married, he may tell her his wife has changed towards him since the birth of their last child or his wife is older now and is not interested in sex with him anymore, or physically she cannot have sex with him anymore or she doesn't enjoy sex with him anymore, or his wife doesn't understand him. The New Age man has a reservoir of excuses to cheat.

He doesn't care one way or another about his disease status or if he has a life threatening disease, or contracts one, or for that matter gets any disease. Remember he is asocial. His attitude, life is a risk anyway. He can as easily get hit by a car as to catch a disease. Also, he figures he is older, so it doesn't matter, or his generation isn't at high risk for contracting a disease, or he'll never get a disease (in denial). If he doesn't care about catching a disease himself, he sure doesn't care if he gives a disease to a woman.

SUMMONING UP
THE AGE MAN

These are cold, empty, heartless and ruthless men, and only warm up in the heat of lusty sex. New Age men only view women as friends if they can get sexual favors from them, emotionally and monetarily exempt. In other words, fucking friends, which is an oxymoron in itself. Would a friend fuck you? NO!

It's all over for the woman just as soon as she sleeps with the New Age man, because this gives him all the power over her. He has gotten what he wants from her, so the game is over. He has won, and sometimes he will let her know immediately in words and actions. He might say, "Well, I have things to do, so you'll have to go now." Or "Thank you." Or "I knew you were hot, but just didn't know how hot." Or "Mmmm, mmmm, mmmm." He'll make an immature wisecrack and make the woman feel less for sleeping with him. He now shows indifference, emptiness and coldness. The table has turned on the woman. She wants love and more from him now, but now he makes the woman chase him for his love since he has gotten what he wants, just sex.

The New Age man will keep a woman off balance. When she starts thinking their relationship is heading in a positive direction, he will throw a wrench into it. His behavior will be adverse in regards to their bonding any closer than just sex. He preys on a woman's weaknesses and vulnerabilities to string along this victim! He now uses these two things for controlling a woman for sexual favors until he dumps her for new prey. At this point, if a woman feels this is where she is in a relationship with a New Age man, be strong and just dump him. Garbage is dumped!! This will throw him off balance, because he has lost control over this victim.

These men also believe and practice these old adages: "One woman, man." That is, one woman at time. "Why buy the cow when the milk is free?" He's clever enough to get it free. "Why have one dish, when you can have smorgasbord?" It's just that sex is easier to get from women these days, because of the sexual revolution of the 1960's. "Women are like buses, if you miss one, you can catch another and another and another."

He expects so much for so little from a woman. He wants her sex, heart, mind, soul and anything else he desires if a woman gets caught in his web of deception and lies, or his big game of trickery. He wants to maintain casual sex with a woman at all costs, as long as it's free of emotions or money on his part. This man is never open or honest about anything, but he is so very obvious about the urgency of wanting sex. If a woman is watching with her eyes wide open she can easily detect this. Go on your GUT FEELING! Don't be fooled by this clever, diabolical emotionally underdeveloped moron, for that's exactly what he is in reality.

ACTUAL STORIES FROM WOMEN OF EXPERIENCE

Dee fell for an old friend of hers by re-acquaintance on the Internet. She thought they had a relationship of love and friendship. When she went to visit him in another state after a year and a half of speaking on the phone together daily, e-mailing each other two or three times a day, and her visiting him several times in another state at his home – Dee confronted him regarding their relationship and his feelings for her. He laughed and said, they didn't have a relationship and they were only friends. She almost lost her mind because she felt used, betrayed, and duped out of her sex without any emotional involvement on his part. His attitude is typical New Age man.

Marla was very open and honest with a man that wanted to get involved with her romantically. She told him she had them lined up for sex only: A lot younger, more handsome, and richer then he was, and she wasn't interested in just a sexual relationship with him. There wasn't a trick this New Age man didn't use, or words he didn't say, to this very attractive woman to get her sex. He even tried to destroy her totally, because he did something very bad to her and she told him she was going to sue him. He used everything she told him about herself against her even to the point of contacting the doctors she worked for and told them she was mentally ill. He is such a monster, he tried to blame Marla for what he did, by saying she had a split personality. He even tried making her lose her state license by somehow convincing all the doctors she worked for that she had a split personality and they all colluded together trying to make her lose her mind. If Marla hadn't been such an accomplished woman they may have succeeded.

Verna loved her husband more than most women love any man. This man chased women to the extent that he could barely afford to support his family. Poor Verna worked as a drugstore clerk her whole life and never had a home – because he never had enough money left over after running around his whole life with every woman he could con into going out with him. Verna died destitute after a life of love and devotion in marriage to a horrid New Age man who couldn't have cared less.

Lisa has a doctor for a husband, but she had no idea she got more than she bargained for with this man. His whole life he used his profession as a way to run around with every woman he seduced. He is always on the way to the hospital delivering a baby. Yes, delivering a babe to the bed of the nearest hotel or motel, whichever is closer. To this day, Lisa doesn't have a clue about her husband's cheating ways.

Lynn has recently married a man and she has no idea he picks up prostitutes on the street. He has certain days of the week he tells his wife he is going away for business, but in reality, he meets with certain prostitutes for a few hours weekly for dinner and sex. Since he has his own business, his wife believes he is doing business. Yes, monkey business!

Monica has a dentist for a husband. When he wants to visit his girlfriend in Mexico or take a new girlfriend on a trip, he tells Monica he is going on a fishing trip or golfing tournament. He'll even go so far as to have flyers printed up making it appear authentic. She has no idea he's bogus as well as a cheat!

Delores married a man that was her high school sweetheart. They had gone together for six years and then married. After they had children he decided to start seeing another woman, unbeknownst to Delores. He continued seeing this other woman for two years by telling Delores he was working until seven o'clock every night. Actually, he only worked until four and spent the extra hours with the other woman. Delores became suspicious when his personality changed. He had great weight loss, started wearing stylish clothes and started drinking and smoking. Finally, Delores hired a detective and found out the truth and why he had changed. She was devastated and depressed for years after realizing his double life! Of course, she divorced him.

A POEM FOR ALL WOMEN ON THE MEND FROM A DEBAUCHED MAN

EPITOME OF A BOAR

Dost thou think thy would stand for follies and deliberate
Acts of contempt proposed… Worst yet make a mockery of
LOVE?
Nay, I think not!
Can you relate to words such as…
Ingratitude, Devaluate, Dishonesty, Cruelty-
And let us not leave out… Inhumane?
Do these words hit home?
For you are what you are.
Intimacy is no more than a piece of paper to be torn in
Half, trashed, and discarded!
Yes…
I've been to the scum of the earth looking for honesty…
Oh…
What foul truth observed there.
How dare thee think I shall tolerate such a diabolical
insult!
The Challenge is over--- Thee are no more than a boar…
To be thrown over thy shoulder and missed.
The façade is ultimately unveiled…
The performance was insufferable,
But achievement was mine---
And…

I'll be subjected no more!
Thy level and disposition is far more superior… just as
high as my heart--- incomprehensible to crass people.
Love and intimacy are life's greatest, insurmountable,
gifts…
And because of this---
Thou are deemed unworthy.
And
History is upon you…
There will be no more
Old Fetid Boar!

Author

WOMEN GET YOUR BRICKS BACK: CLARIFICATION OF THE SEXUAL REVOLUTION

The sexual revolution and sexual equality between women and men is NOT about being a sexual victim or used by men, but rather the equality of having sexual gratification from an orgasm. Women from the past, most all of them, seldom or never experienced an orgasm. However, it was a man's right to be satisfied. It was a woman's duty having sex with her husband. The sexual revolution, in part, is about women being equal sexually as a man, as far as being satisfied. Even today, there are women who do not orgasm. When a woman has sex she should be sexually satisfied as a man usually is. It is a woman's responsibility to know her sexual anatomy to achieve sexual gratification. Compatible partners are knowledgeable and take turns. Sexual sophistication is a responsibility resting with both mates. Also, a man who is a good lover, and cares for his mate, and regards her fulfillment can help her achieve sexual gratification.

The New Age man views the sexual revolution as a means of taking advantage of and seducing women for his own ego, selfishness, and instant sexual gratification. He is totally unconcerned about women in any other way, but sexually. He knows most women are confused in understanding that the sexual revolution is about sexual gratification, and not sexual immorality or women acting as men do sexually, because she is sexually liberated.

Generally speaking, men are the hunters and pursuers. Mankind began here! This is the innate nature of man and his game to be the hunter. Women today are trying to change the hunting game by chasing after men. This is not a natural phenomenon and men know it and are taking advantage of women in hot pursuit of them. Ladies remember infamous names such as: Don Juan, Casanova, James Bond, and Zeus. Today there is a trillion dollar empire built on the exploitation of a new woman for a sexual mate monthly! Arabic men have harems of women and Mormon men have many wives. There are even a number of female animals that lodge and mate together with one male. Taking it a step further, there are infamous male murderers that prey on women. For instance: Jack the ripper, Bluebeard, John Collins, and Ted Bundy to say the least. For the most part, the male species have always pursued the female for whatever reason, not the other way around!

The New Age man feeds off of this very deluded notion some

women hold regarding the sexual revolution and being a liberated woman. He woos a woman to his bed and then makes a woman pay traumatically if she has this misconception and gets involved with him. This is a pity for her. Women who have never been a victim of these kinds of men do not know how horrific they are or can not relate to the women who have encountered the New Age man and have suffered at his hand.

Men in general still view women as cheap if she is sexually promiscuous. Men kiss and tell, or brag to other men, about their sexual conquests with women, and talk behind a woman's back after having sex with her. Women on the other hand usually don't tell. Therefore, there are and will always be double standards no matter what a woman believes, does, or whatever her behavior is regarding sex. As long as there is a dictionary with the definition of words for whore, slut, and words of this nature, there will always be double standards.

Men usually pick a woman to marry him and have his children. Oh, yes a woman can pick a man to marry her, but it's likely it will never happen. New television shows support this by bachelors having their choice of so many women at one time. No matter how sexually liberated a woman sees herself, the man is the one who still and will usually ask for a woman's hand in marriage most of the time. He will buy a ring for her proving it too! By nature men are the hunters and pursuers.

Women, heed the warning signs and wise up before being used up and discarded by the New Age man. Society is yielding to a man's sexual desires by the degradation of women. Many women today

44

have succumbed to the real or fantasized sexual pleasures and desire of men, as many women as quickly as possible. Women acting as men do only cultivate this behavior in men, and voila the New Age man!

The poor in society are women and their children. Women having children out of wedlock is becoming very prevalent in society. Most of these women and children will have substandard lifestyles and life chances or changes. The New Age man impregnates women and doesn't marry them. He may have many children with different women he has not married and vice versa; unwed women may have many children from different men. People are not perfect and the way society is headed is not good for women. Moral decay and the loss of the family unit is an end in itself for any society.

Women are deluded if believing the sexual revolution and a liberated woman is about being amoral, or acting as men do sexually. Woman with this belief have caused degradation for all women in society by stooping down and falling off the pedestal. Women need to get their bricks back and think more of themselves. Prevent making emotionally exempt sex readily available for men, because women are victimized and used up for just sex by these kinds of men.

Make a man work for what he wants. It's likely he will then appreciate and respect what he gets. Make a man love you first, and then let him lust you. This way both win! Men usually like to work for what they want and are use to working for what they have. It's a man's world, but women are superior in that, women don't think about their next sexual conquest perpetually!

A Message
From The Author

After many years of staying home raising my son, I decided going out again and having a life of my own. After getting involved with a few men, there was a realization that men have changed dramatically over the years since I had last dated them. At first, it was incomprehensible, but after many encounters with them and going out with different men, there was an apparent complete pattern of behavior men were employing. I started investigating other women friends and their experiences with men as well, finding out there was a whole New Age of men in society.

Please understand this writing was done in the hope of saving women from the art of the con that many men are employing in society today. This was written through the eyes of women who have had life experiences through the eyes of debauched men. Because there are many facets of complicacy in the lives of men and women, my writing will help simplify the one avenue it addresses for women - understanding the New Age man and the sexual favors con they are employing!

This information was compiled from the personal experiences of myself and from other women I have associated with the last few years. This was written from the frontier or new boundaries regarding today's attitudes of men getting all the sex they can preying on women with the deluded idea of being sexually liberated. Some women have realized there is a New Age man out there in society, but cannot express the manifestation. I am writing about the human animal in respect to gender acculturation, and how this acculturation process manifests itself sociologically in contemporary relationships today. This might be the first definition of the New Age man regarding how they have psychologically evolved in society today.

This information is not in some text explaining this crude manifestation by some psychiatrist (such as Freud), but rather based on men's contemporary attitudes and their capability of employing thought out and learned (through books of seduction) behavior and their ability to apply the art of the con. Besides, this is relatively new and acquired from today's experiences of women trying to have relationships with these kinds of men. This is man on woman behavior, and only women can convey these experiences about men.

As far as I know, there is no science proving this behavior, but only the experiences of women who having endured these men with this behavior - unfortunately for them! There is no sugar-coating for the unconstrained lust some men have for women today, but women have the right to know, providing the knowledge is available. This was written in respect for the woman desiring this knowledge.

I am hoping every woman who reads New Age Man – Con Game Over will be enlightened enough to withstand this diabolical character in society today and enhance her life by recognizing and avoiding him.

EPILOGUE

Lest Ladies Becoming

SHARK BAIT

The ocean is big and the ocean is deep,
If you swim there alone he'll come in to eat…
He swims under the water, so very swift and silent,
OH…
If he gets to close… look out
He's so terribly violent!
The more attention you attract
The more compelled he is to attack,
If you try to fight
This will provoke him to bite!
Don't think you can stroke him…
For that's just what he wants,
Then he can feed and taunt you
With very much flaunt!!!
He'll gobble you down as quick as he can,
Because he is horribly vile
And wants to swim many more miles…
Yes,
He's in the big ocean
And he swims very deep,
You might think he's a keeper,
But he'll eat you up without defeat!
He's a throw back you see for
The character he lacks.
Yes…
He swims in the big blue
And he'll make you think he is true…
But, you'll find out sooner or later he is only a flue!!!
You may think he's your fate, because he'll
Persuade you to mate…
But the reality is you just become his
Shark Bait!

Author

About the Author

Dr. Marilyn Marlow
The Sex Shark Buster!

Dr. Marilyn Marlow has been a professional practicing since 1981. She graduated from the University of Detroit, School of Dentistry; where she was the class columnist for the Dental Monthly Report. She was married to a dentist for five years, and after divorcing practiced her profession full time. When Dr. Marilyn was not working, she was home raising her son. After many years of seclusion, being preoccupied with parenthood and her career, Dr. Marilyn decided dating again. This is when she encountered the New Age man.

www.ingramcontent.com/pod-product-compliance
Lightning Source LLC
Chambersburg PA
CBHW061221280526
45784CB00006B/2573